This book is dedicated to anyone who has ever struggled with their own uniqueness. Lean into it and embrace who you are. —S.Q.

HarperCollins Children's Books, a division of HarperCollins Publishers, 195 Broadway, New York, NY 10007
HarperCollins Publishers, Macken House, 39/40 Mayor Street Upper, Dublin 1, D01 C9W8, Ireland

Fros, Fades, and Braids: A Brief History of Black Hair in America • Copyright © 2026 by Sean Qualls
All Rights reserved • Manufactured in Capriate San Gervasio, Italy • No part of this book may be used or reproduced in any manner whatsoever without written permission except in the case of brief quotations embodied in critical articles and reviews. Unauthorized use of this publication to train generative AI is prohibited and this publication is excluded from the EU's text and data mining exception.
harpercollins.com
Library of Congress Control Number: 2023941329 • ISBN 978-0-06-314427-9
The artist used acrylic paint, paper, colored pencil, and collage to create the illustrations for this book. Book design by Chelsea C. Donaldson and Caitlin E. D. Stamper
25 26 27 28 29 RTLO 10 9 8 7 6 5 4 3 2 1 • First Edition

# HAIR

## CORNROWS  JHERI CURL

## GUIDE

# SEAN QUALLS
# FROS FADES AND BRAIDS

## A BRIEF HISTORY OF BLACK HAIR IN AMERICA

**HARPER**
*An Imprint of HarperCollinsPublishers*

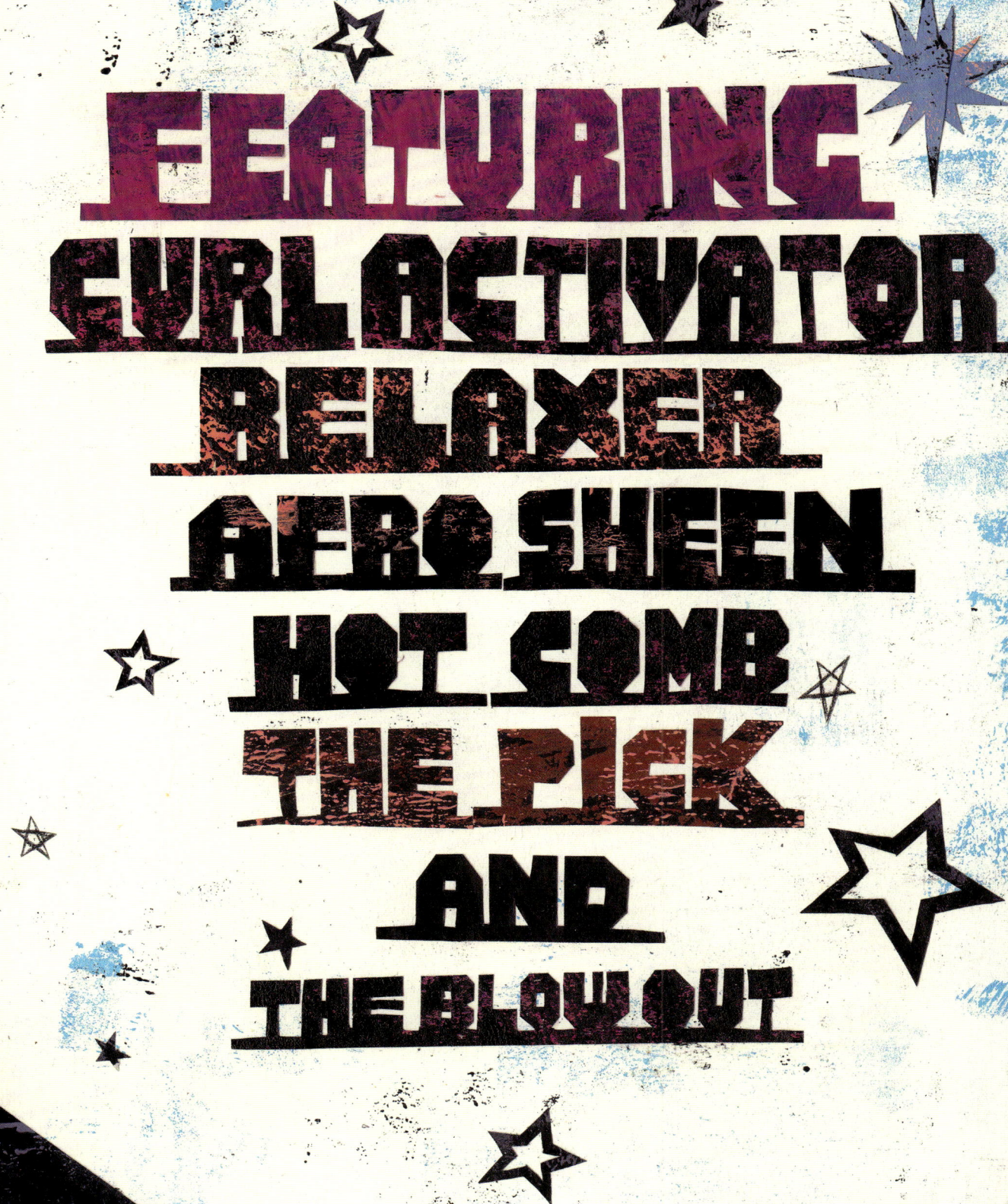

# HAIR, HAIR

It's that stuff that grows on top of your head.
Speaking of that soft and rough, fuzzy stuff,
for many Black people,
taking care of their hair
is of supreme importance.
After all, hair is the highest part of the body and the closest to heaven.

And since it sits all the way up there,
some people consider their hair
a crown.

# *NEW AGE* HAIR GREASE CO.

**Oh, hey there, friends!** Welcome to a little bit of history of Black hair. Let me ask: Where would we be without our hair? Can you imagine a world without it? There are just so many types and styles: wavy, wooly, kinky, curly, brought to you by the same company that created endless waves, silky curls, and other hype for your hair! Yes, you know it! It's the New Age Hair Grease Co. Bringing you the products that give you and your do that extra something special!

**O**ur story really begins with not one but two very special ladies. The first was so special they called her *madam*—Madam C. J. Walker. One of the most famous women of her day, she was among America's first female self-made millionaires. By making and selling her very own beauty products for Black women, she created a hair-raising empire!

But before her rise to fame and fortune, she was a mother struggling to provide food and shelter for her family. Around the year 1900, Madam C. J. Walker began losing her own hair. Who knows why—maybe due to stress or a poor diet.

It was then that she began experimenting with different creams, ointments, and mixtures to regrow her hair. Later she would turn what she learned from that ordeal into a multimillion-dollar business.

At one point, the Madam C. J. Walker Manufacturing Company was so successful that it employed nearly twenty thousand people. Madam C. J. Walker's employees, mostly Black women, sold her products and showed other women how to use the "Walker system" to grow longer, stronger, and softer hair.

And then there was Annie Malone—a businesswoman, inventor, and educator who also made and sold hair products for Black women. She was Madam C. J. Walker's biggest competition. Truth be told, Annie started her business four years before Madam C. J. Walker even launched her company. And believe it or not, guess who was once Madam C. J. Walker's boss? Yes, you got it—Annie Malone. The hair business treated Mrs. Malone so well that she started her own college to teach others what she knew about making and selling products for Black women.

In addition to being a successful businesswoman and the creator of her own hair and cosmetics line, Annie Malone, like Madam C. J. Walker, was a millionaire of the self-made variety. She was so generous, it was said that those who worked for her company for five years received diamond rings as a gift. Mrs. Malone believed that by giving Black women the tools to take care of their appearance, she could help them feel better about themselves and improve their lives.

Both ladies had style—they loved the fancy life, drove big cars, and had grand homes. Despite their competition with each other, they loved to help those in need. They were philanthropists: people who give their time and money to help other people and organizations.

# ANNIE MALONE

Producing hair products wasn't just for the ladies; meet Mr. Garrett Augustus Morgan. Garrett A. Morgan invented a formula to straighten hair. Yup, you heard that right. While working on a solution to make sewing easier, he accidentally discovered a way to bust the bounce out of those tight and tiny curls.

And thus started the G. A. Morgan Hair Refining Company in 1913. He sold his hair-straightening cream across the country to Black people who wanted that "good hair" look. The money that he earned from his hair products allowed him to spend his time inventing other things that he became more well known for, like the three-way traffic light and gas mask.

**R**ight about now, you may be asking yourself, "Why was it so important for some Black folks to have straight hair?" And what exactly does "good hair" mean, anyway? Well, ever since way back in the day, when some people thought it was okay to own another person and work them all day and night without pay or compensation, there's been this talk about "good hair."

You see, most of the people who did the enslaving had straight hair and had the nerve to make the other people take care of it for them. And they imposed a beauty standard of straight hair. Back then, many Black women wore cloths to cover their hair, but they still did their best with what they had to take care of their hair. Even when slavery ended, this idea of "good hair" as loose and straight and "bad hair" as tight, curly, and kinky continued.

# BLACK WOMEN WITH STRAIGHT HAIR

Even before Garrett Morgan made his mix to kill the kink out of curly and wooly hair, other folks had created tools like the straightening comb and flat iron, which were used to transform naps and knots into hair that flattened and flopped, at least temporarily.

Maybe now you know why Mrs. Malone and Madam C. J. Walker are so important to our story. Their products and inventions helped people change the way they looked at themselves. Many saw straight hair as a symbol of freedom and a better life; braided and *cornrow* styles reminded them of the cotton fields and slavery, and many wanted to leave those days far behind.

Once people learned that there was a way to have their curls lie flat and straight, it was like opening a floodgate. Black people across America were saying goodbye to their cornrows and nappy 'fros—straight was in! Black women and men were taking their cottony curls and letting them loose, wearing them long and wavy.

**conk**
/KONGk/
noun:
A hairstyle in which curly or kinky hair is straightened. The conk was a hairstyle popular among African American men from the 1920s to the 1960s. This hairstyle called for a man with naturally kinky hair to have it chemically straightened using a relaxer, so that the newly straightened hair could be styled in specific ways.

# BLACK MEN WITH STRAIGHT HAIR

In homes and barbershops across the country, men started getting their heads conked. The *conk* was a straight style, and the formula was made from potatoes, eggs, and a chemical called lye. This way of straightening hair would later become known as *relaxing*, because the curl relaxed so much, it became straight.

    Conking hair did the trick, but it was also toxic and could make men sick. Hairdressers had to wear gloves, and the concoction had to be washed out quickly, or clients could go bald! Despite the danger, the style still raged on, and people would wear it in big *pompadours* in the 1950s and 1960s. Many famous rock and rollers like Chuck Berry and Little Richard wore it, and so did blues men like Muddy Waters and Son House. Additionally, boxers like Sugar Ray Robinson and even the Godfather of Soul himself, Mr. James Brown, wore this style.

For women, there were hairstyles galore: the *pageboy*, the *bob*, the *bouffant*, the *beehive*, the *bubble*, and the *poodle cut* were all popular in the 1950s and 1960s. Still, many people continued with traditional styles like plaits and braids.

Plenty of men and boys went to the barbershop just to get their hair cut. In fact, visiting the barbershop became a big part of people's weekly schedule, and barbershops and beauty salons became a crucial component of countless communities.

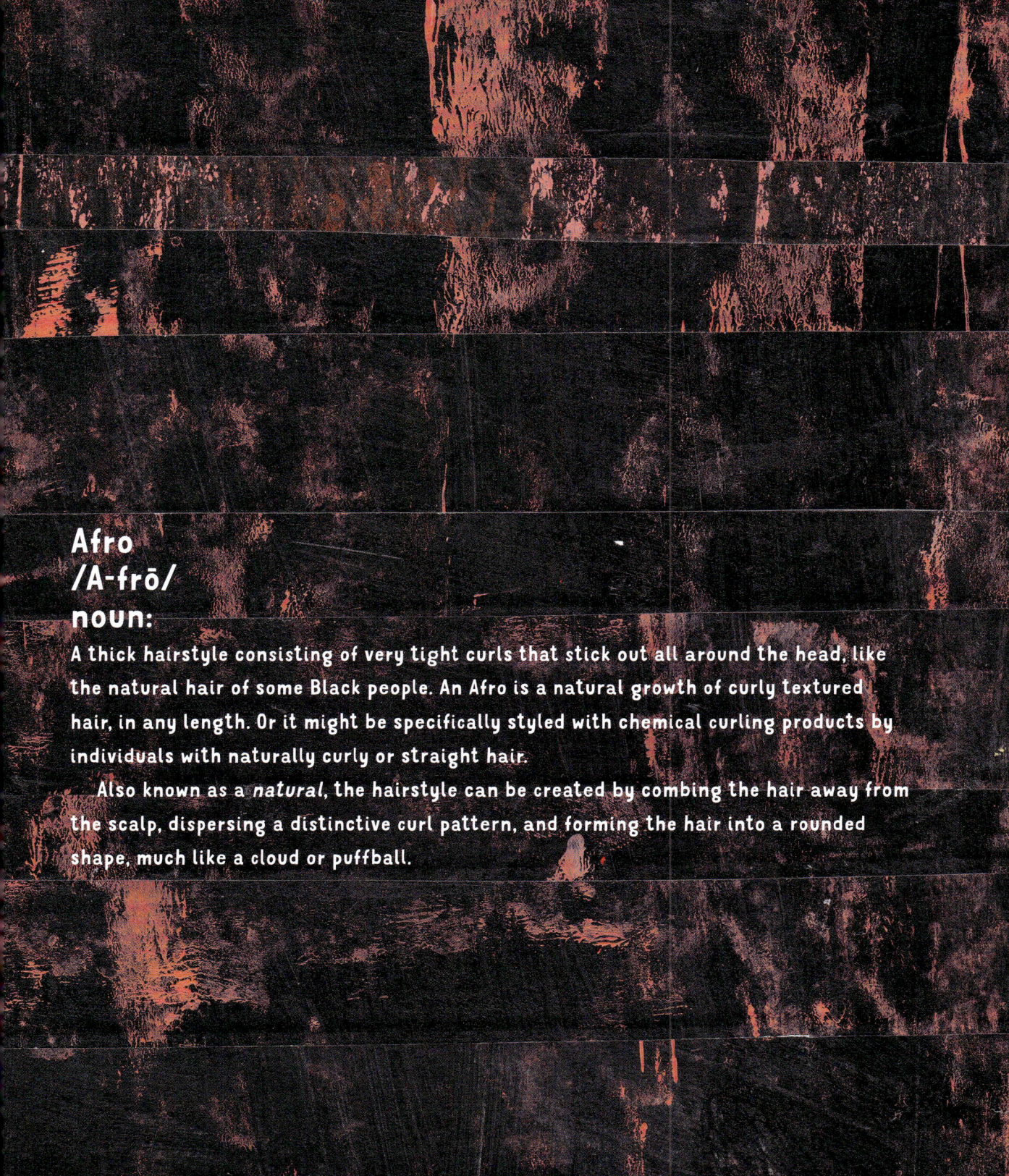

# Afro
/A-frō/
noun:

A thick hairstyle consisting of very tight curls that stick out all around the head, like the natural hair of some Black people. An Afro is a natural growth of curly textured hair, in any length. Or it might be specifically styled with chemical curling products by individuals with naturally curly or straight hair.

   Also known as a *natural*, the hairstyle can be created by combing the hair away from the scalp, dispersing a distinctive curl pattern, and forming the hair into a rounded shape, much like a cloud or puffball.

# THE NATURAL HAIR MOVEMENT

Hair straightening didn't change the way everyone looked at Black folks, and some of the unfair ways of the old days lingered on. Changing their hair from curly to straight wasn't making things any better. People wanted real change! The people wanted to be heard and seen, and that meant being proud of being themselves. Why try to be anyone other than you?

    Some folks saw straight hair as a move in the wrong direction. They started to make their voices heard. People began to embrace how their hair was in its natural state. Phrases like "Happy to be nappy!," "Black Power!," and "Black is beautiful!" became powerful statements that gave people permission to be themselves.

# FAMOUS FROS

And just like that, the *Afro* was born! The 'fro looked like a round cottony cloud, and it was everywhere in the 1960s and 1970s. Men wore it, women wore it, babies wore it too. Soon everyone wanted one! I mean *everyone*. Suddenly folks with straight hair were getting their dos treated so they, too, could wear the natural!

And with this new style came new ways of keeping their hair right and tight. First there was *the pick*. The pick was a type of comb people used to lift and fluff their 'fros high.

And then there was *Afro Sheen*—the spray that kept people's 'fros soft . . . smooth . . . shiny.

Sometimes people would use a brush and a blow dryer to *blow out* their 'fros. The *bigger* the 'fro, the better.

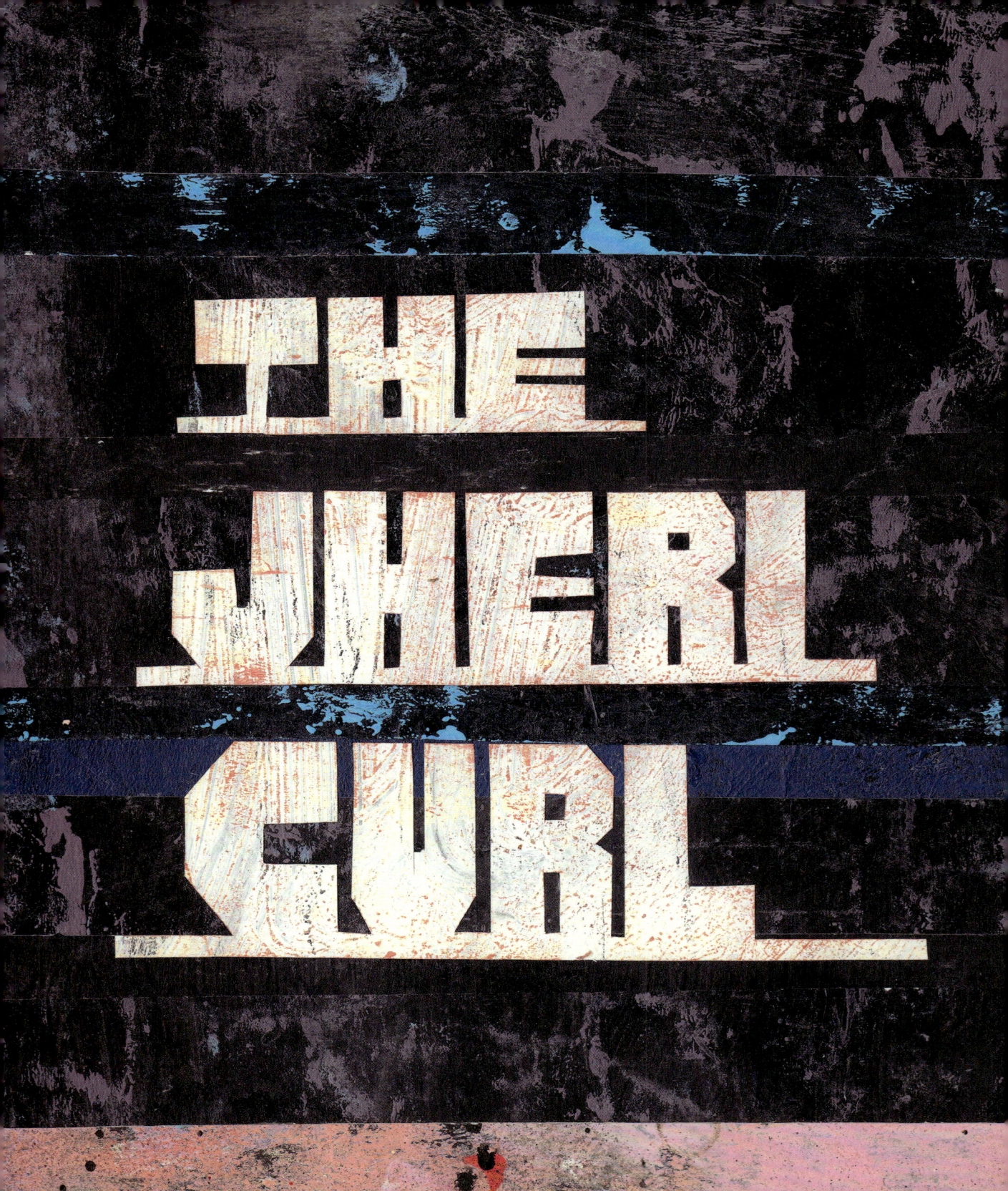

Jheri curl
/Jeh-ree kurl/
noun:
The Jheri curl is a chemical hair treatment that creates loose, bouncy curls with a signature wet-look sheen.

Just when it seemed like the 'fro would be around forever, a newer, curlier look came onto the scene in the 1970s. It was smoother... shinier... silkier. It was a radical change from the Afro. The *Jheri curl*, also known as the *California curl*, was anything but natural. It used a chemical process similar to relaxing that loosened the kink right out of the curls and required a special spray to keep it that way. If people didn't have the money or the time to get it done at the hair salon, eight dollars could buy a do-it-yourself kit to use at home.

# JUICY JHERI CURLS

Once you got the curls, they had to stay moist. *Curl activator* was the juice that kept those Jheri curls wet and juicy. Go a day or two without your activator and your hair would snap back to the way it was. The Jheri curl became known for its wet look. Hungry heads all over were thirsty for the flavor of their favorite activator. Some people wore it curlier, some wore it wavier, but either way, it required a lot of that special sauce.

The style spread like wildfire. And speaking of fire, there was at least one reported case of a famous musician who kept his curls so filled with the oily activator that they caught fire.

In fact, it was this and stories like it that may have led to the waning of the Jheri curl. Other styles eventually started to replace it.

There was the *asymmetrical*,
the *hi-top fade*,
waves,
*locs*,
and *braids*,
but still some people refused to let go of the wet look.

**locs**
/lɑːks/
noun:
Locs are a hairstyle created by twisting or allowing hair to mat into ropelike strands naturally. They can be short or long, thick or thin. The style's origin can be traced back to Greece, Egypt, and other regions of Africa.

When *dreadlocks* began to appear on people's heads in the 1970s and 1980s, it was a shock to many. Formerly, mainly people known as Rastas wore their hair that way. They followed a religion known as Rastafarianism. People didn't know what made Rastas' hairs stick together in the ropelike locs—some thought it was dirt, glue, or wax. Some people actually used beeswax to make it work. But really, dreadlocks were another natural style, like the 'fro. And once those locs began to grow, you could just let them go or style them however you wanted.

There were
short locs,
long locs,
hi-top locs,
mohawk locs,
thick, skinny, and mini locs.

Locs (sometimes called dreads) were the new natural. And like the Rastas, many people who wore locs were getting into natural, healthy foods and lifestyles.

**fade**
/fād/
noun:
A hairstyle in which the hair is cut to gradually grow faint and disappear, usually on the sides and in the back.
   The fade originated in Black-owned barbershops and has become the popular term for an aggressively tight taper. Hair at the sides and back is cut as close as possible with clippers, and fades, or tapers, down from almost any length on top.

**T**his cut has been around ever since the 1930s, when the electric clippers were invented. Back then, people called it a crew cut or a high and tight. The style quickly caught on with the military, but it was really Black barbers who elevated the look. It became better known in the 1980s and early 1990s as the *fade* or hi-top fade when rappers like Kid 'n Play, Bobby Brown, and Big Daddy Kane wore it. The hi-top fade was really an exaggerated version of its predecessor, with a higher and more defined top. It looked like a crown.

**braids**
/brādz//
**noun:**
Strands of hair, usually three or more, which are interlaced to create various patterns. They can be worn short or long, close to the scalp or hanging from one's head. Also known as plaits, braids can be woven into specific styles, like cornrows, box braids, and French braids. They can be piled on top of one another to create a bun, styled as knots, or worn loose.

Around the same time as locs, *braids* became more popular. But braiding had been around for years. Mothers would braid their daughters' hair, and even some men wore cornrows. Yet now people were getting their hair braided like never before.

Like locs, braids come in all different sizes. But unlike locs, braids are not always natural. Often, the person getting their hair braided wants it to be long, and to achieve this, more hair is added. Hair extensions can be made of real or synthetic hair.

Some people loved the idea of having much longer hair almost instantly! Folks were excited. Many made the trip to the beauty shop and just hours later walked out with longer hair. This is called weaving. People could also get their straightened hair extended as well.

*Extensions* and *weaves* became a major part of the already growing business of hair care. For people to keep their hair happy and healthy, they needed to have some sort of moisturizing product in it. Otherwise, it would become dry and break. Depending on the style, someone may use oil or grease, conditioner, or a spray. Many people use them every day!

And all those products add up! Sales of Black hair care products generate *billions* of dollars per year. Now that's big business!

# DON'T DO IT!

If you're not familiar with all this stuff, and the care of Black hair is new to you, you might be so bold as to go out and try to touch somebody's hair without their permission. DON'T DO IT!

First of all, you have no idea what kind of products someone may have in their hair. What if they're sportin' a Jheri curl? *Surprise, surprise,* you get a handful of activator! Oops!

Second, show some respect—ask first, or better yet, throw someone a compliment.

What's next?

Seems like the more styles change, the more ways there are that people can express who they are!

Nowadays you can see folks with all sorts of hairstyles, all kinds of looks—long, straight, short, kinky, curly, wavy, nappy, or natty. All that matters is that you are doing you, being true to yourself, and not trying to be anyone else.

Some people have decided that straight is the only way for them. Others love keeping it curly. We have unlimited ways of strutting our stuff, showing the world who we are. Whatever you do with your do...

# AUTHOR'S NOTE

Why a book about Black hair, specifically Black hair in America, right now? Black people have a deep and complex relationship with their hair. In the United States alone, Black people spend billions of dollars on grooming and hair care products annually. People who are not Black often chalk it up to vanity, which is a highly inaccurate and insensitive assessment.

*Fros, Fades, and Braids* seeks to tell the story of Black hair in America, starting with Madam C. J. Walker and hair-straightening, and ending with what's happening with Black hair today. The art includes portraits of some of the key players in the creation of the Black hair industry, as well as some of the personalities that made notable styles like the conk, the Afro, and the Jheri curl famous.

Hair care for Black folks is a way of declaring one's freedom of self-expression and personal identity. *Fros, Fades, and Braids* is my love letter to Black hair and is for anyone who wants to know more about it!

Photo by Ginger Qualls

**SEAN QUALLS** is a Brooklyn-based artist, illustrator, and author. His work is a mixed-media combination of painting, drawing, and collage. He has illustrated many picture books, including *The Idea In You* by Questlove; *Before John Was a Jazz Giant*, which received a Coretta Scott King Honor; *The Poet Slave of Cuba*, a *Bulletin of the Center for Children's Books* Blue Ribbon book; *Dizzy*, an ALA *Booklist* Notable Book and a *Kirkus Reviews*, *School Library Journal*, and *Child* magazine best book as well as a *Bulletin of the Center for Children's Books* Blue Ribbon book and an ALA *Booklist* Editors' Choice; and *Emmanuel's Dream*, which was a Schneider Award winner and an Amazon Best Book of the Month. You can find him occasionally DJing in and around New York City. Visit him at seanqualls.com.